Escape The Office Tower

Donita Fowler

www.donitafowler.com
www.vestedinterestgroup.com
www.themeasurabledifference.com
www.businessmasteryunplugged.com

This book is dedicated to all the people who work from a home office, or coffee shops or park benches.

I am one of you.

You are my tribe.

Donita Fowler is a content producer and digital marketer – her clients include business owners who want to enhance their online presence through social posting, blogging and website content.

www.donitafowler.com

Alongside her husband, Vince Fowler, they also own Vested Interest Group – a boutique business-coaching firm located in Calgary AB. Together they help entrepreneurs and small business owners build a business that allows them to live life on their terms.

www.vestedinterestgroup.com

A growing component of their coaching practice is an online membership website called Business Mastery Unplugged. Vince and Donita co-created this digital program to allow entrepreneurs to learn in an online (membership) format. Each month provides podcasts, worksheets, book recommendations and bonus material.

www.businessmasteryunplugged.com

Together with a small team of volunteers, they have also created The Measurable Difference. It is a bi-monthly speaking seminar focused on helping small business owners. They have different speakers come and share their story from the stage, giving real, authentic advice to the audience. Everyone who speaks or attends believes in sharing knowledge without expectation.

www.themeasurabledifference.com

Prologue

Welcome to my home office success story. It's been quite a journey for me to get here. My success didn't happen overnight, and it won't for you either. I'm going to guess that if you bought this book, either a) you work from a home office, or b) you are about to.

Don't worry – everything in this book is going to lay the foundation for you to have success in your home office. Even if you think you are ready – this book will show you *how* to work from a home office. I've worked from a home office for most of my career – and once I put certain strategies and systems into place, my life got a whole lot simpler.

Table of Contents

Chapter 1 How It All Started

Chapter 2 Mindset

Chapter 3 Outside Looking In

Chapter 4 The Default Calendar

Chapter 5 Developing A Routine

Chapter 6 Making Connections

Chapter 7 Staying Connected

Chapter 8 Home Office At Last

Chapter 9 You Are Ready

Chapter 1

How It All Started

This book is designed to help people who work from home become more successful. Take what you will from the advice and tips that I write about, but understand one thing. These are my own ideas and strategies, there is no one-way to be successful. There are many ways, but I am going to show you what worked for me. Working from a home office takes a little tweaking from the brick and mortar office. But, once you learn the tricks of the trade (so to speak) you won't want to ever go back. You will ride the home office train like a Harley Davidson motorcycle with the wind in your hair – never looking back.

Let's begin by taking a step back and learn how this all began. It's June 2003 and I've just graduated from University with a Communications Degree.

Perfect. Now what.

I, like many others in my situation, threw my resume into space and hoped (and prayed a little) that someone, anyone, would like what I had to offer. About 3 weeks go by and I got an interview for a sales job. So, I put on my best suit and with my resume in hand, I had the interview and subsequently, I got the job. Sales Professional – that was a title that I could get used to, and I felt pretty good about myself – everything seemed like it was falling into place. And it was, except for one little problem – the job was based from HOME!

What? Home office? What does that even mean? Does that mean I need to clean out my spare room and try to assemble a desk, and put up a bookcase? I was terrified that my boss was going to come to my house, take a look at my spare room, make me take down my Mel Gibson Braveheart poster from 1995 and tell me to take a hike.

The reality is, my boss barely even asked if I lived in a house or a condo, or if I even had room for a home office. Reality is, he sent me a laptop and a cell phone, told me to install a fax line and wished me luck in my first few months. 4 days later my business cards arrived and sure enough, my name and title were on those cards – so, it must be true. I'm officially a Sales Professional, working from home.

I previously worked in a brick and mortar office and I liked it. I will admit that there are a few things I would have done differently if I had the chance. I would have put my cubicle next to a high performer, and I would have avoided the water cooler talk, and I would have always taken my uneaten lunch home at the end of the day – but all in all, I enjoyed (or thought I did) working in that conventional office space. I wasn't *scared* to work from home; after all I had come from honest beginnings, small town Saskatchewan. I had pretty good work ethic, but I also did have a clear picture of what my first real job would look like. And it looked like an office tower on the 18th floor, and (in a perfect world) I had my own office. I know what it didn't look like. And, it didn't look like the house I shared with 2 other girls, with a closet in my *new office* that had my spare winter jackets in it. Deflated? A little. Scared? A little. Anxious? Absolutely.

I had a lot of training for my new job, but I had no training to set up my home office. 2003 wasn't really the time of 'Google' or 'Wikipedia' – so I got some advice from other business professionals, but it turns out that sometimes adapting other peoples bad habits isn't the best thing to do.

So, I bought a used desk, set it up and was ready for my first day. Looking back on all of that now, I see how unprepared I really was for those first few years of working from a home office. I was naïve and I was not prepared – so, if this sounds like you – don't worry. This book is going to put you light years ahead of where I was when I began.

In the following chapters I'm going to outline what it takes to actually set up a home office, and how to succeed by working from one. I've spoken to many professionals on the advantages and disadvantages of working from home – everything from hours they work, to the people that keep them sane during the lonely days. I'm going to take you inside the mind of a home office organizer so that you can see how setting up your office can affect how productive you are during working hours.

The most important message this book conveys is the mindset of someone who works from home. A home office can be a place of great beginnings or tragic endings – and the road to get you there is all based on you. There is a learned skill in working from home, and it can be great – I hope that after reading this book, you are able to set up your home office and work comfortably and efficiently from it.

Chapter 2

Mindset

Working from home has a certain *network marketing – get rich quick – no need to really work* stigma attached to it. From now on I'm going to refer to it as a *home office space* or *mobile office space* – no need to get your mind thinking that this isn't a real way to run a successful business. Truth be told, companies can save tens of thousands of dollars by having a home office / work from home option for their employees.

Imagine the hours spent on driving to and from work each day – those are valuable hours that are better spent with family, friends or (imagine this) getting your work done early – no need to burn that candle at both ends. The only real difference for someone who has home office space vs. the corporate office space should be the commute to and from work. Now, there are going to be little tweaks that you are going to have to make along the way - some definite lines will have to be drawn, and some hard and fast rules will have to be set – but you have just given yourself 10+ hours / week more with family, friends and yourself. Name me something that you can do overnight that will give you 40+ hours / month back in TIME. One of your most valuable resources that can be drained is TIME, so getting some back should be enough reason to go to your boss (if you have one) and tell him you need this *home office space* option.

I know I said that we are going into the mindset of a successful home office space employee / business owner. Reality is that it should be the same as anyone (employee or business owner) wanting to succeed in life. There shouldn't be different work ethic, shouldn't be different goals or success's and there really is no reason to have a different outcome. You are just making your time at work blend a little easier with your time away from work.

1. Successful people DO, they don't make excuses. (No matter where their office is).

If that makes sense to you, perfect. I once heard the saying 'it's not your resources that will make you successful, it's your resourcefulness'. It takes a certain amount of resourcefulness to work in that home office space. Example: your fax line stops working, rings busy when it's not – whatever. You can't just call the IT department and have them come up and look at it. You need to become the solution to the problem. In reality, you are your own solution – for almost everything that goes wrong. Flip side. You are the reason that almost everything goes right. You need to develop an independent outlook on your work. What does that mean? You need to ask yourself 'what do I need to do to get this done' each and every time you come across an obstacle. And my suggestion will be to say 1 of 2 things every time something goes either wrong or right.

1. What do I need to do / implement so that does happens again?
2. What do I need to do / implement so that doesn't happen again?

Nothing comes out of complaining that you can't do something. In fact, in our business *can't* is a very bad word. You simply don't use it. You ask for help, you seek out answers and you cope. You don't say *I can't* anything. But, when something does happen that slows down your day, or makes you want to quit because things are getting just too frustrating – implement something so that it doesn't happen again. If an invoice doesn't get paid, or a customer doesn't get a return call – make sure you implement or systemize the process so that it doesn't happen again. One of my advantages in working from a home office is that my business partner (and husband) Vince Fowler works from a home office as well. This can make it either *easier* or *harder*. We choose the first one. So, together we have become stronger working from home. But, that is not saying we don't have bad days, everyone does.

> "Bad days are going to happen no matter where your office exists. So it isn't if a bad day happens it's when a bad day happens working from home. Thus, it's important to recognize when that's happening and have a mechanism in place to get your mind back into the game. How a person gets mentally back on track will vary from person to person. For me, different things help. From a random quote that I have taped up on my wall to a quick walk around the block. Research has proven time and time again, a physical break is necessary to maintain creativity and productivity.
>
> It can be difficult working from home because of the isolation. Maybe the solution is moving yourself away from the isolation, and moving yourself to ta coffee shop or a gallery – something where it changes the environment.

Another solution is to call a client, obviously not to say your lonely, but as a touch-point. The act of doing something good for others has a rebound effect and it uplifts the mindset and spirit of you. Doing something good for others, even if it's just touching base with a client is just that.

In extreme cases of frustration, a lot of those strategies might work. But I've learned that if I'm in a really bad headspace, and I cant shake it no matter what I do. Then the solution is to give myself permission to be in a bad mood. Give myself a certain amount of time to unwind. In the past its been working out, watching a Netflix program, watching TEDTalks – the key to this is to set a stop point. I don't care if it's thirty minutes or 2 hours later, or the next day. Set that time to reset the brain to mentally recover from that stress. And, I would encourage exercise and play to be a part of that recovery."

Vince Fowler, Speaker & Business Coach, Vested Interest Group

2. <u>This isn't a holiday. Don't treat it like one.</u>

Time and time again, I've spoken to home office workers and they say that the first few months almost lost them their job. Reality is – they almost lost the job themselves. It's very easy to get into a bad routine of getting up late, not showering and putting on your work clothes, making that one last browse of Facebook – STOP IT NOW! We are in a world where the home office space is going to become more of an option as time goes on – so we need to stop acting like we need a babysitter and start acting like successful business people.

Everyday requires you to get up at your regular time, shower, dress and go to work. No different in a home office environment – other than your commute to work is merely a walk down the hall or a trip to the basement. Trust me, you are still going to work – very hard most days, but your mind will be clear. Don't take that extra time you have in the morning to sleep, or have an extra long breakfast – take the time to make one more client call or dig up one more referral. Use that time to your advantage as much as you can.

Danilo Terra, a leasing expert, worked from the office tower for over 10 years before starting his own successful business and basing himself out of his home office.

> *"The transition was not hard. It was a breathe of fresh air compared to the long commute or icy bad roads. I had more time to concentrate, with less distractions (co-workers), etc.*
>
> *Sleep-in a little? It doesn't happen, I find. Generally I put in at least an hour before the children get up and get ready for school. Knowing I have only an hour to accomplish at least one big goal for the day before the household awakens, really helps me get up and get to it. Wanting to provide great service to my customers is a big motivation for getting up in the morning. I'm not doing them any favors staying in bed, and for me if it affects*

other people, it's plenty of reason to get up and get to work. In the end, serving my clientele well serves me well.

I find that getting showered, shaved and dressed before I start work is a key element to setting myself up for success for the day. Once the phone calls start and email emergencies start, you won't have time. Then, you're caught with your pants down (literally, lol) when the workflow hits. You never really find your groove for the day, I find. I also find I have at least one appointment for the day, so you may as well be ready for it the moment you hit your office in the morning".

Danilo Terra, President, Danilo Terra Capital Strategies.

The benefits of working that extra 10% - 15% will increase your bottom line 30%+. Moral of the story – working in that home office space isn't a holiday – so don't treat it like that. Treat your home office with respect – this is where you are going to make client calls, send emails to prospects, earn new clients. This is where you are going to make money to feed yourself and your family – a home office is a real office. Make sure you treat it like one.

3. <u>The Mental Benefits of NO Commute.</u> Get your TIME and SANITY back.

There will be no listening to the traffic report on the TV before you head out to take your hour – hour and a half commute downtown. The frustration levels of someone who has just had a bad commute to work is 76% higher than someone who 'time travels' to work. Think of this as your own time travel invention – now smile, and know that your clear head and mind will allow you to work a little smarter each day – from home. Have you ever had a call right after you've driven in terrible traffic to work? It's not pretty – you've probably taken your frustration out on your customer or worse yet – your potential customer. It takes you all morning to tell everyone in the office about the jerk in the white Honda prelude that wouldn't let you merge and almost sideswiped you. It's a major time waster. Let go of that frustration once and for all – let your commute be about 30 or 40 seconds and let the only traffic be a walk by as your dog lays down for his/her morning nap.

Your savings on fuel, wear and tear on your car and most of all wear and tear on your mental state is a major benefit to working from the home office. On average, people spend 1 – 2 hours / day travelling to and from work. Add that up over a year, you have just gained 9 weeks of your life back each year. Are you skeptical of my math? It's ok – here it is: 1.5 hours per day, X 5 days per week X 48 weeks per year (I've given you 4 weeks of actual holidays) = 9 WEEKS. Wow, that number is huge in a lifetime – too huge for print, but you can certainly multiply 9 times the number of years you have left to work.

Working from a home office gave Danilo Terra back some of his sanity, and allowed him to accomplish more. And even allowed some of that time to be spent back with his children and family.

> *"The commute is a big one for me. I used to spend hours commuting. Now, I can hit the ground running the moment I am ready to do so at the home office. I have way more hours to accomplish what I need to. My family benefits the most I feel, no more late suppers or after school care. I can work the same amount of hours (or more) and still be home to turn on the oven or pick up the little ones.*
>
> *Avoiding the rush hour commute helps me accomplish more and run my household more effectively. I believe all parts of life have to run well to be successful or feel that way. The lack of commute (or being able to commute to meetings during parts of the day that are better) sets me up for success at home and with the business. As a single father, there isn't a lot of slack, and not being stuck in traffic really helps me meet the obligations of the family and my clients. The lack of commute truly is a winning*

time strategy. Not to mention, it allows me to divert that mental energy (and cash resources) to other things or people".

Danilo Terra, President, Danilo Terra Capital Strategies.

I've just covered 3 major points to someone who needs the mindset of working from a home office. It's not hard – it's actually quite simple.

1. Don't make excuses, just DO IT!
2. This isn't a holiday; so don't treat it like one.
3. Make the most of your time that you save from no-commute.

Believe me, if you can master working from a home office – your outlook on work (whether you are an entrepreneur or an employee) will change for the better – and you will become more successful because of it. Getting your time and sanity back is one of the most rewarding things in a home office environment.

Chapter 3

Outside Looking In

It is going to take a little bit of time for everyone to realize that working from a home office doesn't look any different than working from a corporate office. I tell my audience that developing a space that is professional, sensible and usable will be the difference between success and failure. Not everyone has the luxury of having an extra room or den that can be used as a home office, so you have to be creative. That is just a reality in today's world. I have worked with clients on every level when it comes to creating your home office space and I have broken it down into 3 major categories.

1. Be Professional

I know that we all have distractions in that home office space, but talking to a million dollar client while your kid is screaming, dog is barking and doorbell is ringing – not cool. You are giving home office workers a bad name. Take yourself away from the chaos of everyday life when you are speaking to clients. It's that simple. You need to be present with your clients, so don't confuse your home office space as time with your kids, or an excuse to only have a half time nanny.

I used to have people actually say to me, 'you are so lucky to work from home, you can have your kids with you all of the time.' Really? Is that what people think? There is no way that I could run a successful business with a 4 and 6 year old underfoot. Can I make exceptions? Absolutely. But as a rule, I always have my kids in school or dayhome during the day.

I know that life happens, kids get sick, nanny's go on vacation – and that is fine. You will have a back up plan for those types of life's distractions (or if you don't, you need to make one) – but day-to-day, you need to give your clients your full attention. Go to another room, go on the front step, take a call in your car – do whatever it takes to make that client call your best one ever. Remember, someone else out there is trying to earn *your* customer all of the time. And if the one trying to earn their business doesn't have a barking dog or crying child in the background, you might have just sealed your own fate. You need to treat your customer like the one that wants to steal them away. Always be professional, present and productive when you are dealing with clients from your home office space.

Christy and Jesse Switzer run a very successful renovation company out of their home. Other than being on site, their home office is where they run their day-to-day business. Oh, did I mention that they have 3 small children as well? Christy didn't start out with childcare, but she soon moved towards it.

> *"I do have child care during office hours. For me, this was an evolution. I started out working when my kids napped and after they were in bed, and I'd use the free childcare at my gym to make calls (picture me sitting in the hall beside the squash court with a laptop on the floor). Over time my kids napped less and the business grew and I was drowning. Like, this is not fun, what were we thinking...drowning.*
>
> *It was never my intention to "do it all" but I'll admit I tried, if only because I was nervous about letting go of time with my kids. In the end I arranged childcare so that I could improve the quality of my time with both my kids and my business.*
>
> *My business, and my sanity, would not have survived if I hadn't separated work and home. And as a bonus, my children now have a better example of what a good life*

looks like.

I now have three days of childcare each week. For me, this is the balance I was looking for. And that's just me, I understand that every parent will have to figure this out for themselves.

I keep regular work hours on my workdays, I don't tidy the kitchen or do laundry. I'm working. I've learned to be ruthless about that. If I don't stick to my schedule I'm either texting at the zoo or I'm emailing a client at midnight on a Tuesday. And that's just not the life I want."

Christy Switzer, People Person, I Know A Guy Renovations.

I think that Christy is like a lot of us, hoping and praying that we can do it all. But, we can't. And that's ok. You need to find the balance that works for you.

I once had a co-worker that would always take important calls in his car. I thought it was brilliant. He was away from the hustle of his busy home (with kids and dogs) and he was able to focus on the call he was making. No need to get fancy, you just need to get the job done.

Don't talk about the fact that you work from a *home office* – just call it your *office*. Very few people will ask where your office is, don't lie if it comes up – but stay professional and just call it what it is – your office. For safety reasons, I always suggest getting a PO Box close by for your mail, and your return address on invoices. You can usually have the box number as a unit number, so an example would be: Box 21006 actually becomes Unit 21006. So the full address would look like this: Unit 21006, 645 Riddler Drive, Calgary AB. T4F3C2. It keeps you professional, and you don't have to give out your home address on mailings, and invoices.

Ideally, you do have an extra room or den that is set up as your office. Somewhere that you can open the door, step inside, close the door, and 'boom' you are at work. Being at work needs to create a feeling for you – and that feeling needs to happen each and every time you step into your office. Be it a feeling of success, a feeling of professionalism – whatever the case may be. That needs to be created for you to be successful. In many cases, companies are going to require you to have a separate lock for your office space where client records or confidential information can be secure. Keep that in mind when you are creating that space.

2. Be Punctual

Throughout this book, I am going to continue to remind you that being punctual at your home office is critical to your success. If you start work at 8:30, don't stroll into your office at 8:45. You now have 15 minutes to make up on the other end of the day – the time when you will be longing to get out of this office and have some time with your family.

I'm sure some of you are rolling your eyes right now and saying to yourself *"that's WHY I work from home, so that I CAN be flexible"*. I would argue that being flexible means working 10-6 or 12-8, it doesn't mean working less hours or your success will be affected.

Here's another example of 'do the math' when it comes to cheating on a few minutes here and there. If you show up 20 minutes late each day – you are cheating yourself out of 80 hours / year of work. That's an extra 2 weeks of work. Working from a home office doesn't mean you want to make less money or be less successful – but cheating on a 'few' minutes here and there will definitely affect your outcome. Bottom line; be punctual.

Be on time and have set hours. Work with a default calendar – I'll cover that in the next chapter.

3. <u>Be Practical</u>

This one has a few meanings for me when working with clients. Amazingly enough, 'practical' can mean a few things for many people. I've had people tell me that it is 'practical' for them to work from their kitchen table. Okay. I've also had those same people tell me that they go days without getting any work done. Or, their pile of work just grows, and the mess starts impeding into other areas of the house.

Sometimes you just need those outside eyes to tell you that you've crossed the line from home office space, to home 'where ever' space. You need to actually develop a space where mentally you have just stepped into your office, and I don't believe that starring at your kitchen counter and remembering that this weekend you need to clean out the fridge is the way to do that. Now, if you are someone who needs to use the kitchen table for a short period of time, I would suggest spending half of your day in a coffee shop environment. It gets you out of the house; most have free Wi-Fi now days – and it forces you to enter into a new environment. It gets your creative juices flowing. I actually suggest to people to block off some 'coffee shop time' most weeks in their default calendar. It just gives you a different space to work in – I'll go over that in deeper context when we cover the default calendar.

Being practical means that you need to set aside a 'practical' working space, one that looks and feels like an office. You should be able to transport that office to anywhere in the world and it would feel like an office. I've had clients that take green painters tape and section off a portion of their living space for their office when a spare room isn't available. They've set up bookshelves, room dividers – whatever it took so that they felt like they were stepping into their office, a much different feeling than you should have when you sit at your kitchen table.

The other side of practicality comes with the amount of paper and stuff that an office can acquire. You need to set up some sort of filing system, buy a shredder – whatever you can to DE-clutter that space. Think back to your corporate office days and how much that back room was filled with stuff. Old toner, boxes of contracts, files, swag from years gone by. That needs to not exist when it comes to your home office. Our highly technology focused business world uses drop box, shoebox, digital filing or email. There really isn't much of a need to keep every piece of paper that comes your way. Sometimes, buying a simple scanner and scanning your paper to dropbox is an easy way to keep the clutter down as well.

I know a lot of successful entrepreneurs that use a professional organizer, just look for one in your area. One of the ones I've worked with and I would recommend you look up is Think

Productive. Dawn O'Connor is a Productivity Ninja and she will come in to your home office and help you get organized. You can find them at www.thinkproductive.ca.

A professional organizer will take your office to a new level of organization and with that comes natural success. No office clutter, no mind clutter. I have had clients that work from their kitchen table because they have literally outgrown their office. Stop, drop and shred. One or two sessions with an office organizer and they have their life back – well, they have their office back.

> *"It's a personal preference for messy or tidy spaces. Some of our clients do actually seem to thrive with a bit of clutter. Certain types really enjoy having 'high visibility' of their stuff (and they worry about things being 'out of sight and out of mind'). But I think it's a fair assessment to say that the majority of us breathe a sigh of relief when*

we minimize the volume of paper, declutter our desk and truly know where to find what we're looking for – without having to memorize that our GST form resides in the top third of paper stack on our desk.

It's important not to waste mental energy trying to remember where stuff is in a chaotic environment. Simple systems to keep important information and office supplies handy will relieve your brain of a burden, freeing up mental capacity to be used for more creative problem solving and deeper work."

Dawn O'Connor, Productivity Ninja, Think Productive Canada.

I am a firm believer in what Dawn teaches. I can't help but think that if you have a cluttered desk, you probably have a cluttered mind. Having a clean workspace just allows you to be more creative at work. And creativity is an important part of any entrepreneur's daily life. Even if you don't think you need to be creative, if you had to grab a client file and run out the door – if you have a clean office / desk then you know exactly where it is. Always expect the unexpected – and having a tidy workspace allows you to plan for that.

Chapter 4

The Default Calendar

Looking back over my years of having a home office, I wish someone could have shared this tool with me a long time ago. There is a constant struggle with working from a HOS that includes

   a) Laundry vs. client calls
   b) Dishes vs. paperwork
   c) Vacuuming vs. getting your expenses done

You get the picture. And trust me, any good sales person working from that home office space can rationalize that doing housework will give them time in the evening to get some more work done. And, I do know that can work – sometimes. Believe me, it's the exception – not the rule.

Think back to your University days (or any time a major project or presentation was due). When was your house the cleanest? When were you the most domestic goddess you have ever dreamed of? That's right. Exam time or deadline time. Well, in a home office – sometimes exam time is all of the time. And it can get away on you really fast.

Most of the time when you use your daylight hours to do housework or personal errands, that time is not made up on the other side. Even if you can take some evening hours to work on a few things, you can't make calls and no one is going to answer your emails. You can definitely do expenses, or work on some low level administration – but your optimal working hours are going to be during the day, during the week. This is your *customer facing* time. They are going to be decision-making hours for your customers. Utilize that time.

If you are someone that needs to have Monday and Wednesday mornings free to do something personal (child care, go to the gym, volunteer) that's ok – but the key is to plan for it. And in this chapter, I'm going to show you how to plan for it by using the number one tool that a lot of people miss – the Default Calendar.

I've been very successful in business working from a home office, but the one thing I've always used and always relied on is my <u>default calendar</u>. Of course, I've had days – even weeks where I've had to juggle and move appointments and I've felt like I haven't followed any kind of routine. But, give yourself a break – life will always get in the way, its up to you to get it back on track.

Let's dive right into what a default calendar is and how to successfully use one.

My business-coach-husband Vince Fowler introduced me to the Default Calendar. Why is that important? Because I didn't trip upon a default calendar, I was told to use it by people who help others succeed. If anything in this book is system and process tested – it's the default calendar.

Your Default Calendar is exactly what it sounds like – it's a *default* schedule put into a calendar format for you to follow. The success of a default calendar is going to depend entirely on your ability to actually use it. Trust me, I know clients that use a default calendar all of the time – and they love it. But, everyone who uses a default calendar goes through some 'introduction' phase and getting used to it isn't always fun or easy – it is worth it though. You make your default calendar in excel format – I've given you the downloadable format at www.donitafowler.com.

Once you have it complete, you transfer that calendar to your online calendar (mail, Google, etc). Then you transfer your days from the default name into what the meeting or phone calls are actually about.

I've broken down building your default calendar into 4 easy steps – follow these and you will have a calendar that works for you and your business.

<u>Step 1.</u>

Make a list of all of the activities that you need to complete

    A) Daily

    B) Weekly

    C) Monthly

Next, you need to give that activity 'hours needed' to complete the task, and the number of times you need to visit the task.

Make a list of 'daily, weekly and monthly' visits to that activity. The list will be long – and that's ok, we are going to work on shortening it in a little bit. Let's call these your 'Routine Activities'. Make sure you leave nothing out, include everything including marketing your business, updating social media, client emails, research – everything. What I usually suggest to clients is that they make a list one week of what activities they are doing – and the time that it takes them to do it. If you have some activities that you do monthly, be sure to add those as well. For example, I only send my expenses and bank statements to my bookkeeper once a month.

We are going to use this list a few times, but for now – we are going to use it to build your Default Calendar. Here is an example of what the list would look like.

- ✓ Update Buffer (twitter, fb, LinkedIn) – 3 hours.
- ✓ Marketing – 4 hours
- ✓ Client Retention – 5 hours

- ✓ Client Experience – 8 hours
- ✓ Writing – 10 hours
- ✓ Financial Review – 4 hours
- ✓ Connection Meeting – 10 hours

As you can see, when you break down these activities your days, weeks, even months are going to become a lot more focused on what needs to be done.

Step 2.

Put your month into an excel worksheet. Either follow Week 1, Week 2, Week 3 and Week 4 – or put in exactly what days you are working – either way works. This is going to depend on whether you are in charge of your time (business owner, entrepreneur) or if the company you work for dictates your time (employee). If you are an entrepreneur, use the Week 1 – Week 4 format – that way you get a Week 5 a few times a year. That now becomes your holiday week. If you work for someone else, this becomes more of a challenge because they are going to want to dictate some (if not all) of your time. That's ok too – the important thing is that you list the activities and give them a time slot.

I know to many of you, this seems relatively simple. It is simple. That is the key to the default calendar, it's not about being overly complicated or hard to implement. It's about being able to create something simple to put into practice immediately in your home office business.

Step 3.

Take the *routine activities* and your new excel sheet and start plotting in what needs to be done and where. There will be 2 tabs on your sheet, so make sure that you are going back and forth between the two so that you don't miss anything on your routine list and so that you don't forget anything on the actual excel calendar. Here is an example:

Week 2	Monday
9am	Team training call
10am	Client Email Follow up
11am	Client Appointment set from last week
12pm	Client Appointment set from last week
1pm	Marketing - Social Media
2pm	Prospect Calling
3pm	Update CRM
4pm	Update CRM

Don't forget that in your routine activities tab, you have already said how many times something needs to be done per day, week or month. As you put the activity into the excel calendar, mark an X by it so that you know it's been given a time slot. This part of the exercise might take the most amount of time. You need to make sure of some simple things when deciding what times of the day/week to do something. If you work with a lot of clients that live in a different time zone, make sure you allot for the time difference. I have calls / clients all over Canada, so I always give my Eastern Canada clients my morning time slots – and my West Coast clients get later times in my day. Personally, I'm a morning person so I stick to doing my creative tasks in the morning (if possible). There are days when I struggle with focus in the afternoon, so I stick to routine tasks and repetitive activities during those time slots.

Another example would be: every other Wednesday morning, you need to take you son to an activity and then drop him off at the dayhome. So, you can get up extra early on that day and get a few emails done before he gets up. And then you always know that you work abit late on those particular Wednesdays as well. As long as you prepare for some life events to happen during your home office workday – and you have a plan, you are going to be able to fit them in. It's the unexpected life events that can take us for a tailspin. That brings me to the final step in creating your default calendar.

Step 4.

Be prepared to move blocks of time, but make sure you give it another time slot. I always encourage people to have 2 – 3 blocks of time per week where you put *unexpected activity*. This can allow for you to have an unexpected meeting with a new alliance, or if you need to spend a little extra time with a staff member. I've heard many professionals say, "Expect the unexpected" -- so putting blocks of time will allow for just that.

Let's say it's Monday morning, and you just got a phone call from a pretty big new client and he wants to meet Tuesday afternoon. You have blocked that time off for [Marketing – Social Media Strategies], but you can't turn down your new client.

It's simple, just take that Marketing block and put it somewhere else. The key is that you actually put it somewhere else. You can't ignore an activity, even if it seems pretty minor to you. When you say yes to something, you are saying no to something else. I'm going to repeat that one, *when you say YES to something, you say NO to something else.*

Now, I'm sure you are thinking to yourself that there are going to be times when life gets crazy and you just can't fit in that activity anywhere. WRONG. Always find somewhere to put that activity. These kinds of adjustments to your calendar are what is going to be the difference between average and awesome. It's better to reduce the time that you have given the activity rather than get rid of it altogether.

Vince Fowler coaches business owners and helps them start to live a life on their terms with their business. One of the ways that he is able to help with time management is with the default calendar.

"The default calendar is ideal for someone who is either new, maybe they just left the cubicle and now they are working a business from home. Or maybe they are someone who appreciated structure. Either way a default calendar can be extremely helpful. Think of a default calendar as a way to categorize an activity. If you just wake up and wonder what you are doing today – then typically people just do busy work. They wake up, head to their office, and open email. Next thing you know it's 3 hours later and nothing has been done. That can be a bit of a frustrating feeling. In the midst of addressing the onslaught of email (or Facebook, or LinkedIn) a customer calls or a vendor calls.

The shiniest most pressing activity gets addressed first. This is frustrating if it happens 1 day; it's downright insanity if it becomes a routine. And I'm sure with a lot of start-ups, this has a risk of causing their business to fail. The things that they should be focusing on just aren't getting focused on.

So, creating a default calendar is addressing a number of routine activities that happen in the business owner's life, whether it's weekly, bi-weekly, and quarterly. An example would be social media, emails, customer contacts – these categories give you a clear idea of what you should be focusing on. Those time slots that you fill with categories are designed so that you focus on all areas of your business – and not just the immediate pressing ones."
Vince Fowler, Business Coach & Speaker, Vested Interest Group

Now that your default calendar is complete (and you understand the importance of it) you should be able to start your week with a clear vision of what needs to get done. I am always telling people to revisit their default calendar and make adjustments where necessary. Sometimes as your business evolves you are going to need to spend less time on certain activities and increase activities on others. Maybe you don't prospect as much as you used to, but now that time is given to client experience. I will often encourage people to actually block off a time each month to review their default calendar. This is one project that will never be complete.

Get used to using the default calendar – it becomes your insurance policy for your time. And again, it's not written in stone – so adjust whenever you need to. Just remember – you can't delete but you can move to another block of time.

Chapter 5

Developing A Routine

Now that you've completed (or at least started) your default calendar and all of your routine activities are planned out – let's dive into the real truth when it comes to making something *routine*. I continue to tell my audience that their success is going to come from the routine that they can implement into their home office business.

I'm going to give you a sport analogy. I like sports, and I think there are a lot of similarities between business and sports. The real difference between an *amateur* athlete and a *professional* athlete is routine. Once you reach the professional stage, you want to have all of your routines so embedded into your daily living that it is just normal to you. Each athlete plays a sport – but the *professional* trains harder, eats better, sleeps more, uses more resources – and all of that takes them to the next level. Ask yourself, do you want to have an amateur business, or a professional business.

Routine is important in any business, but it is especially important in a business where you truly are your own boss in charge of your own time. Even if you are an employee, and you have a direct report – they don't live at your house, they don't visit you every day – and they certainly aren't going to dictate what you need to do every waking hour. When I first started at a home office, I didn't have any real routine. I just started my day, and ended my day – sure, there were things in between but I didn't actually feel like I got much done most days. Looking back, it was because I didn't have any routines, there were no set-in-stone activities that I did. Routine lets you become proactive not reactive in situations – and being proactive will let you set the tone with your customers.

Today, social media (namely Facebook) is a time sucker. You can waste hours upon hours looking at photos of your friends wedding photographer's cousin's vacation last summer. I know you have. So *stop it!* Sure, you can have a block of time each week to work on social media for your business <u>in your default calendar.</u> But, during working hours – stay off of social media sites for personal use. They will steal hours from your life that you won't get back.

Routine is a very simple concept, although many people seem to try to complicate it. According to some definitions of routine, it means:

"Commonplace tasks, chores, or duties as must be done regularly or at specified intervals; typical or everyday activity".

And truthfully, order is what you are striving for in your business. Some of the routines might be as simple as reaching out to three new clients per day. Those *new client calls* will be in your default calendar so you aren't going to need to guess what time you are making those calls. Setting a to achieve list is a great way to get results fast. Do you want to make 10 calls each day or do you want to book 3 appointments? There is a BIG difference in those two ideas. It might take you 50 calls to get 3 appointments, or it might take you 6 – either way you get 3 appointments and that is the main objective. To be successful you are going to need to set *Achieve* lists and forgo the old school thought of *TO DO* lists. Simply put, "DOING" isn't going to make your numbers – "ACHIEVING" is going to get you closer to success.

Setting up your routine might take some time. You really need to be able to look at your marketing strategies and determine which ones are actually making you money. It comes down to the 80/20 rule. 80% of your activity is giving you 20% of your result – so you need to be able to look at that 20% result and switch it to 20% activity. That will free up 60% of your time to focus on effective activity bringing in more results.

I encourage people to use a default calendar in order to start creating routine around activity. Author Brendan Bouchard says that "10,000 hours" is what it takes to make you an expert in something. You can take that one step further by saying that those 10,000 hours are doing *routine* activities every day. It takes some more time than others to see the benefit of routine, but that is going to be the difference between good and great when it comes to your results.

Do you ever have those days where you KNOW you accomplished something, but you just can't put your finger on what that accomplishment was. I would argue that you don't have a lot of routine, and you are basically spinning your wheels looking for results. It won't happen. Sure, you might hit one or two home runs – but consistently you won't succeed without routine. Don't even try. Remember, routine is the difference between amateur and professional in business. I find routine to be the key to productivity. With that, however, I think it's really important to look at routine in a positive way. I don't see routine as doing the same thing everyday. That just becomes boring drudgery and if that's all I'm doing, I might as well go get a job somewhere. I see routine as structure that allows me to make the time for, and stay focused on doing not only what I have to do, but what I want to do, too.

David Mead is a professional speaker & writer, and he works from a home office. David makes a direct link between routine and discipline.

"Working from home presents some additional challenges. It's often easier to let go of routine at home because we can be easily distracted by the TV, that sprinkler that just needs to be fixed real quick, the child who has the day off from school, or a myriad of other normal distractions that naturally pop up when we are in our home environment. Routine comes from discipline and working from home simply takes more discipline. One thing that helps me stay focused and avoid the distractions that always arise is remembering what I'm working toward. Beyond the daily task list I have, I constantly remind myself of the world I'm working toward. That perspective makes it easier to leave that sprinkler alone till the weekend and stick with the routine I've set for myself."

David Mead, Start with Why

Your *routine* might be calling existing clients, but with the use of the default calendar you have created a list of activities under that routine. They could include follow up with existing clients, referrals from existing clients, customer experience, customer rewards etc. Once the routine is formed, feel free to tweak the activity to fit in everything that you have assigned. You aren't looking for a Groundhog Day experience, but you are looking for activities that produce results. And then you have to do those activities again and again.

Routine will help you with consistency in your business. It will give you structure which is what you are ultimately looking for in success. The scary part for most entrepreneurs or business owners (or sales people, or marketing people..... or people of any kind) is that the get bored really fast – and if that is you, then the thought of routine is extremely scary. You can't think of the routine as something that will take over any spontaneity that exists, but merely as a framework for the work that needs to be done.

> *"For me, setting expectations, both for myself and for my family has been a great help. It's not that I'm militant about my work hours or that I will ignore my family between 9 and 5. However, the expectation is set that my workday begins at 9:00. As part of my routine, I always (well, almost always) shower and get dressed as if I were going to drive to another location for work. Going back to the idea of structure, I usually have something booked in my calendar for 9 am, which helps me ensure that I'm at my desk and ready to go for the day.*
>
> *Part of that structure and routine is also scheduling some free time or time to think...or not. Every day I schedule 10 minutes to do nothing. Yup, nothing. It's not exactly meditation, but it's a chance for me to sit with my eyes closed and try to free my mind of all the thoughts that*

want to bombard it with what needs to get done, who I need to call, what I need to say, the event I have coming up, and everything else that wants to penetrate my consciousness relentlessly the rest of the day.

Productivity, to me, is not filling every minute of every day with something to do. It's also taking the time to sharpen the ax, decompress and clear my head so that I can have a rested mind and more focus.

It's sounds counterintuitive perhaps, but I've also incorporated some flexibility for the unknown into my routine. For example, I rarely lock my office door unless I'm on a client call, etc.. I don't want my wife or kids to feel as though they can't come in. Because I've done a pretty good job of setting expectations, this works out well for me. The flexibility piece comes in when, for example, my son gets home from school and wants to come into my office to give me a hug and say hi. Part of my routine, although it's not scheduled in my calendar, is to allow for these kinds of occasional, important interruptions. Even though I may be temporarily interrupted, after that one minute interaction, I can get back to the task at hand with peace of mind, rather than worrying or feeling bad that I pushed him aside because I was busy being productive. We all have our version of this type of interruption. Be prepared for it and consider building it into your routine."

David Mead, chief of what's next, Start with Why

Chapter 6

Make Connections

One of the biggest mental hurdles in working from home is just that. You are working from home, alone, all of the time. And this might sound a little bit over the top – but the loneliness in working from home is a motivation crusher. Sure, you can go to client meetings and you can call a coworker or colleague in another city and have quick chat. But, the majority of your day is going to be alone – and talking to your keyboard or steering wheel. The loneliness is sometimes a deal breaker for some people, unless you are able to find a way to overcome it.

Matthew Kimberly is an author and speaker, and finds that you need to be able find a way to combat the loneliness – and is probably different for everyone.

"I've always lived in urban areas. Never more than 10 minutes from a coffee shop. I've never found, though, that coffee shops were particularly conducive to working: far too many distractions.

So ... to avoid the plague of loneliness I'd do two things every single day: first, I'd escape the house for a coffee or stroll around the neighborhood at least two or three times a day. Sometimes only for 15 minutes, sometimes for an hour or more. A change of scenery refreshed the mind and allowed me some human contact, even if it was only with the barista.

Secondly, I'd include talking to somebody I *wanted* to talk to - not the bank manager or insurance broker - as frequently as possible. Although "pointless" chats can be a distraction from focus, they're also part of what makes me tick. I'd rather take the distraction and get energized".

Matthew Kimberly, Author and Coach, matthewkimberly.com

I've done a lot of research when it comes to finding groups of people that just want to have some human interaction throughout their day. And really, there isn't much. But I do have a few tips for you.

1. Find 3 favorite hangouts. Whether they are coffee shops, or diners – make yourself a regular and go there often. I know a lot of business professionals that start or finish their day at coffee shops. I often do my writing at coffee shops and I find that even though I'm not always having conversations – it's nice to be around other people. You will soon notice other professionals that are doing the same thing. You get to know the wait staff, the owner, and the regulars. It's just nice to have someone notice you are there and give you a friendly smile.
2. Find a Chamber of Commerce. Every large city has a Chamber of Commerce and they will run events weekly

that you can attend. They will also have a member directory that you can find other chamber members to connect with and perhaps develop some sort of mutual business relationship. The catch? There is a cost – it typically runs between $600 and $1500 / year depending on the type of membership you want but that can be money well spent if it gives you an outlet.

3. <u>Go to Networking Events</u>. Go online to Eventbrite or Meetup and look for networking events in your area. Again, this might sound overly simple – and that's because it is. Networking events are usually full of people wanting to network – but you need to choose your events wisely. Sometimes these networking events are actually full of people just wanting to sell – and that isn't really what you are looking for. But, on the flip side you can usually walk away with 1 or 2 coffee meetings booked for future weeks. Here's a hint, go to the networking event ready to listen. Listen. Listen. Listen.

All day long. If you really want to have an impact on your business, listen to what others are saying. That will make you stand out.

4. This one is my personal favorite – actually <u>join a professional group that meets regularly and has accountability</u>. There are a few of these groups (well, quite a few) but you can usually attend the first few at no charge and then decide if that is what you are looking for. Make sure that the group you choose is in alignment with your business goals, some of these groups tend to be full of people 'looking' to sell, and that is not what you want. Attending the group's meeting a few times before joining is going to be your key to choosing the proper group.

Some examples of these groups are BNI, CBWN, or Probus. Those are just a few – there are tons available – the catch is that there isn't a ton of good ones. Be sure to take advantage of the 'come for free' offer to see if it's what you want to join.

There is a 'hidden elephant' in the room when speaking with home office employees – and that is that it can be very lonely. No one wants to admit that – they think that it sounds childish or immature to admit that you have no one to speak with (other than your boss and/or clients). The sad fact is that there is no real solution to this problem, other than packing your calendar with networking events, and even that won't necessarily allow for the contact that you are looking for.

I always tell my audience to do something during the day that will increase your heart rate and get you pumped up, take a walk at lunch, go to the gym for an hour or so, take a yoga class. Do something that will take the place of an energizing conversation – because that might not be available to you. I've even had people tell me that they always listen to talk radio and that gives them something to listen to and engage with. You will need to find what works for you – and it might not even be on this list – but you are going to have to sit still long enough to find what works for you.

I would also encourage people to connect with groups on LinkedIn (and in certain cases Facebook). These groups are full of people who are in the same boat as you – and they usually are looking to connect with others. Use them as a resource and develop a rapport with them – these groups are good outlets throughout the day and connecting with them might just give you the connection you need. If you can't find the group you want or need – create one. Put it out in cyberspace and see who joins – you might be pleasantly surprised by who is looking (much like you were).

Don't think that it is just beginners that feel alone, or have to network to build their tribe of people. Bob Burg is an accomplished speaker and author for over 30 years and he still finds that connecting with others brings value.

> *"I believe that Networking - when approached correctly, meaning that you are focused on brining value to others - is a huge source of powerful and productive connections. All things being equal, people will do business with, and refer business to, those people they know, like, and trust. When it comes to meeting people with whom you can establish and cultivate these types of relationships, there are few ways more effective than networking."*
> *Bob Burg, Author and Speaker, burg.com*

The real key here is the old saying "the less you do, the less you want to do" – and that is true with working from home. If you haven't been out in weeks, you will make up any excuse to NOT go to that next meeting or next networking event. Give yourself a number each week of meetings, or events that you want to go to. Put these directly into your default calendar. This number can change each week but it will give you something to strive for and it will get you out of the office.

Chapter 7

Staying Connected

We have covered what it takes to *get connected*, but one of the keys to your success is going to be *staying connected*. In the beginning of any relationship (and your business or employer is that relationship) it's easy to stay connected and engaged. It's when the long days, brutal hours and stressful moments come up that your true self will appear.

I don't know if there is an easy way for anyone working from home to stay connected other than realizing that you need to do so. Using a personality test can help you understand your strengths and weaknesses as an individual. It will allow you to find out your highs and low's when it comes to a work environment.

I suggest using a DiSC profile – because it gives you a personality type in normal situations and then again in stressful situations – for both personal and work placements. Once you know if you are a dominant, or supportive personality – you can find out what you need to tweak in your schedule to make sure you are making the best use of your time. If you want to take a DiSC personality test, visit www.vestedinterestgroup.com to find out more.

There are 2 types of people, introverts and extroverts. If you don't know which one you are, just ask yourself how do you recharge? Does being around people recharge you? If this is true, you are most likely an extrovert. Or does being alone recharge you? If you answer yes to this question, you are most likely and introvert.

Why is this relevant? Well, if you are an introvert to start with you are going to have to be extra vigilant when it comes to working out of a coffee shop or public place. You will find it much easier to work from the quiet confines of your home, but that isn't going to be the most successful place for you. You are going to need to get out of your comfort zone to keep your creative juices flowing. I know this because I'm an introvert and sometimes the last thing I want to do is go and write from a coffee shop, but I also know that those times are when I need to. Whatever your personality type, you just need to be able to identify what your strengths and weakness's are.

Bob Burg is an introvert, but still likes having access to virtually connect with others.

> *"I guess I'm lucky to be an introvert. Having a home office is perfect for me as I very rarely feel any type of loneliness working this way. Then again, having access to social media means there is always someone to connect*

with in the event a twinge of loneliness does hit me. And, of course, nothing stops anyone working from home from going out to their local Dunkin' Donuts, Starbucks, or other public place where they can work and also be around the energy of others when they feel the need to be."

Bob Burg, Author and Speaker, burg.com

And on the flip side, if you are an extrovert you are going to go a little stir crazy if you can't be around people most of the time. Your home office will seem like a prison sentence to you, so you are going to need to be diligent at booking client meetings and working from coffee shops.

Understand that there is no right or wrong answer here. We are who we are and knowing our makeup just makes us easier to understand. If you are a seasoned home office worker you will know what you need to do each week to make improvements and just get better and better. If you are new to the home office environment, you are going to need to keep that default calendar close and follow it to the letter until you get comfortable with small changes.

Your success is going to depend on your ability to follow routine – and not get lonely and bored. Boredom will creep into your days, no matter how busy you are, with a home office.

Chapter 8

Home Office At Last

This book is mostly geared towards business professionals that already work from home, and how to be more successful. But this chapter is going to provide you some information on approaching your HR department with some Home office solutions for your current position. Or, it will encourage you to start that business that you always wanted to, but the thought of working from home is just too overwhelming. Trust me when I say it isn't.

Many business professionals have had experience at some point working from home. Either they had outside meetings that day and starting from home was easier, or a sick child prevented them from going in that day – whatever the case, it will have give you an idea if working from home is an option with your position. If it is, here are some strategies to discuss with your current employer.

1. Email Response Time

    Working from home will allow you to customize your working hours to the time zone that you are trying to communicate with. If you are emailing people who are in a time zone 2 hours ahead of yours, and it is crucial that you get responses, you can start your emailing 2 hours earlier. You can really design your day to be customer friendly. You can be available for your customer when they need you to be. It's not realistic to think that you are going to be in the office every day at 6 am – but if you worked from home, you have just cut your commute by about 99%. So, starting at 6 am is a lot easier to think of doing. I knew a client who worked from home 3 days a week because her client base was in a time zone that was 2 hours ahead of hers. She couldn't access the office at 6am, but she could work from home. It was a great solution for both her and her clients.

2. <u>Staggered Implementation</u>

This one has worked for many employees trying to work from a home office. For some, the part time option is one that seems to be the best of both worlds. Let's say you start with 2 days a week, and you keep track (to the letter) of what your days entail.

> How many emails?
> How many responses?
> How many phone calls?
> How many sales?

Keep track of everything and present it to your boss. You are going to have to be careful here. Don't let it be so different working from home that it looks like you don't work from the office. But be sure to highlight the distractions – water cooler talk, waiting for the photocopier, no parking spot, etc.

In many cases the part time option is what works best for professionals. They can design their schedule to work from home on heavy administration days, and from the downtown office on heavy meeting days. It really is something you would want to present to your HR department.

3. <u>Cost Analysis</u>

This is one that you might not be able to do on your own, but you can certainly reach out to your supervisors for help. There is a cost per employee – and by taking that number and multiplying it by 5, and then by 48 you will be able to see the cost your company has by keeping you in the office (assuming you have 4 weeks of holidays).

Now, there is going to be an initial cost for a Home Office Space set up, but once that is taken care of there will be a significant savings to your company. Most companies give a one-time bonus of $500 - $1000 and it's up to you to use that money wisely to set up your home office. Even with that one time bonus there are a lot of factors that contribute to a home office saving for companies. The big one is the rent / lease on buildings. More and more big companies are moving out of that prime downtown office space and moving their employees to a home office.

4. <u>Employee Retention</u>

This one is often overlooked. If you speak to any business in today's world, one of the top four struggles in business is hiring. Letting employees have the option to work from a home office environment can keep them working for you longer.

Having that option is going to let employees coming out of maternity leave an option that would let coming back to work easier – which is a reason that most don't go back to work, or find a job closer to home. Taking this one step further, employees with children don't want the 10 – 15 hours of commute time each week away from their families, and the home office is an option that works.

Whatever the reason that you are presenting this to your employer, be confident in your approach. Be honest. Be transparent. State the facts, and then give options. Whether it's a few days a week, or a few days a month – let your employer know you are flexible and you want to make the situation work for both of you. It might take some time, but it will be worth it in the end.

Chapter 9

You Are Ready

I hope that you have found the stories and strategies useful enough that you are able to work from home with confidence. There isn't a magic pill that will make working from home easy, or make you more successful. You will need to develop routine, and stick to that routine day in and day out.

What I've done is laid some foundation for you with structure, calendar, and mindset. It is up to you now to implement all of these things. It isn't going to be easy at first, trust me. That 2 o'clock *need to get out of the office and watch TV* gremlin is going to be pretty convincing. Don't be fooled. If you can be pretty productive working 4 hours a day, imagine your success working 8 hours a day.

Consider yourself one of the lucky few that have the opportunity to work from a home office. There are definitely perks, and sometimes don't be afraid to cash in on those perks. Do you need to distress and golf on Friday afternoon? Then take the time, but just remember to make it up somewhere else. You can't be successful if you don't put in the hustle. Remember that.

Once you are able to define your skills when it comes to working independently, you will be able to make that default calendar work for you. It isn't always easy to start using a tool like a default calendar, but once you have routine around doing it, my guess is that you will feel very lost without it. Your default calendar can be the only thing that really dictates your time. Because, really there is no other person or thing that is going to be with you in your home office telling you what to do.

It's up to you. It always has been. Everything in this book will turn out badly if you don't implement it. In fact, it just won't turn out. At all. You will read it, and then go back to how you were before. Unproductive, uninspired and working from home. Please don't be like that. Implement something from my book, do it one at a time. Don't get overwhelmed. After all, this home office thing is a way of life, not a short lived mini-series.

Good luck, work hard and seize the opportunity. I did, and it worked out well for me. Now, it took me a few years to get there but you have this guide to help you.

Acknowledgements

I'd like to thank the business owners who took time out of their schedule to give to me.

- Vince Fowler, vestedinterestgroup.com
- Danilo Terra, daniloterra.com
- Christy Switzer, iknowaguyrenovations.com
- Dawn O'Connor, thinkproductive.ca
- David Mead, startwithwhy.com
- Matthew Kimberly, matthewkimberly.com
- Bob Burg, burg.com

Lastly, I'd like to thank you for taking time out of your day to hear what I had to say. #gratitude

www.ingramcontent.com/pod-product-compliance
Lightning Source LLC
Chambersburg PA
CBHW072230170526
45158CB00002BA/833